CONTENTS

ENERGY

What is energy?

A famous scientist, James Clerk Maxwell, said "Energy is the go of things". Energy gives the go for the rocket to blast off, it gives the go for the yacht, and makes the wheels go. Animals need energy to push and pull. Where do you think the energy comes from?

Everything we do needs energy. We walk, run, skip and jump. We cannot see energy but we can see it working. We see it working when things move, and we see it working when things change. Look at the pictures. Which things move? Which things change? Energy makes all these things work.

Sometimes we call doing sums or writing, work. In science, work has a special meaning. Work is done when something moves. Things can be moved by pushes, pulls, or twists. Look for energy at work in the world round and about you.

The words energy and power are often used as though they mean the same thing but, they are not the same. Energy provides the go for the work. Power is how fast that work is being done. For example, the power of a car is how fast the energy in the petrol works to move the car.

FUELS AND ENERGY

Doug Kincaid and Peter Coles

Macdonald Educational

How to use this book

First, look at the contents page opposite. Read the chapter list to see if it includes the subject you want. The list tells you what each page is about. You can then find the page with the information you need.

If you want to know about one particular thing, look it up in the index on page 31. For example, if you want to know about a solar furnace, the index tells you that there is something about it on page 22. The index also lists the pictures in the book.

When you read this book, you will find some unusual words. The glossary on page 30 explains what they mean.

Series Editor
Margaret Conroy

Book Editor
Daphne Butler

Production
Susan Mead

Picture Research
Suzanne Williams

Factual Adviser
Alan Cooper

Reading Consultant
Amy Gibbs
Inner London Education Authority
Centre for Language in Primary
Education

Series Design
Robert Mathias/Anne Isseyegh

Book Design
Julia Osorno

Teacher Panel
Catherine Daniel
Lynne McCoombe
Ann Merriman

Illustrations
Robert Burns Pages 12–13, 14–15, 18, 19, 20–21, 28, 29
Julia Osorno Pages 6–7, 8–9, 11, 16–17, 24–25, 26–27

Photographs
Cover: an oil refinery
Sally and Richard Greenhill: 7
Central Electricity Generating Board: 20–21
ZEFA: cover, 10, 15, 16, 22–23 centre, 23 top, 23 bottom, 24, 25, 27

Which of these things are using energy? Can you think of other things around you which use energy? Which things move? Which things change?

Children need a lot of energy. Think about the things you do for which you need energy.

Energy sources

Where does all the go come from? There is energy in coal and oil, wind and water, and in food and drink.

Nearly all our energy comes from the Sun. Plants cannot grow without the Sun's energy. We use plants as food and so do animals. Food gives the energy to live and work. The Sun's energy of long ago is stored in wood, coal, and oil. Materials which store heat energy are called fuels.

The Sun causes our weather to change. We use the wind and moving water as sources of energy.

There are other sources of energy which have stored energy, such as chemicals, batteries, magnets, and atoms.

In the past we used sources of energy in a different way. Wind was used to work windmills that ground the corn to make flour. Wind provided the energy for the sailing ships on their great voyages of exploration and trade. The moving water of streams and rivers gave the energy that worked the waterwheels. These wheels drove the machinery for the early factories. Some sources of energy we use are fairly new, but other sources have been used for a long time. What sources do we still use today? Do you think that people living in other countries use the same energy sources as we do?

Look at the pictures. Which of these show stored energy? Which of these show energy of movement?

Here are some sources of energy. We cannot make energy, nor destroy it, we can only change it. The go happens when we change energy.

Energy forms

Remember, energy is the go of things. But, energy is never used up when the go happens, instead it changes from one sort of energy to another.

There are several different sorts of energy which are usually called forms of energy. The main forms are:

1. Heat
2. Movement
3. Chemical
4. Electrical
5. Magnetic

6. Light, radio, and X-rays
7. Sound
8. Nuclear
9. Gravitational

Heat is a form of energy. Most other forms of energy eventually end up as heat energy. The heat from this bonfire warms the air and gets spread out. We cannot use the energy any more.

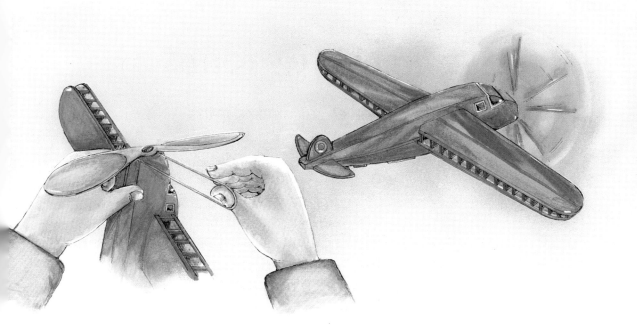

When the elastic is twisted, energy is stored. This energy changes into energy of movement when the elastic untwists and turns the propeller.

Some forms of energy can be stored. Coal and oil are found in the ground and both have stored energy. We can change this energy into another form of energy and make the change do work for us. It can make electricity which can drive a train. The train then has energy of movement. Stored chemical energy in the oil or coal has been changed, first into electrical energy, then into energy of movement.

You could make a model aircraft and use an elastic band instead of the engine. You wind up the elastic. Then the energy stored in the elastic turns the propeller. The aircraft flies. Where does the energy come from? Was it from you and your food? The food grew. What energy made it grow?

Energy chains

When we use energy, it changes from one form to another giving us go. Several energy changes can link together making an energy chain.

Doing the washing is part of an energy chain which starts with the Sun. Long ago the Sun helped to grow great forests. The trees died and over millions of years became coal. Now people dig up the coal. This needs energy some of which is human energy. At the power station, burning coal gives heat energy which makes water into steam. This drives the dynamos to make electricity that cables carry to our homes. The washing machine needs electricity to heat the water and wash the clothes, then Sun and wind dry the clothes. A lot of energy is used during the building of a washing machine, more than the washing machine uses in its whole lifetime!

During each change of energy form some energy gets lost as heat energy.

Think about a space shuttle flight. The stored energy of the fuel is used for blast-off. It makes heat, light, sound and movement. Then the shuttle rides round the Earth not using any energy. When it returns to land through the atmosphere it heats up. The heat energy is spread out and lost in the air.

These pictures show an energy chain. Long ago the Sun's energy helped forests grow.

The trees died and over millions of years turned to coal. Today we mine the coal and use it to make electricity. The electricity runs the washing machine and then the wet clothes dry in the sunshine.

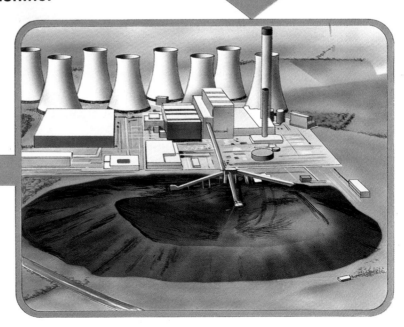

13

FUELS

Coal

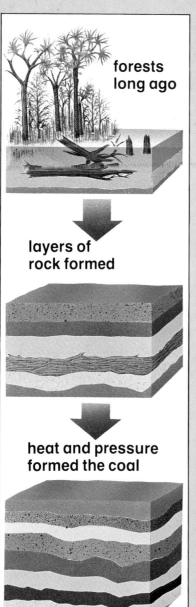

forests
long ago

layers of
rock formed

heat and pressure
formed the coal

A fuel is an energy source which can be changed to give heat energy. Coal is one of the most important fuels. It is called a fossil fuel because of the way it was made from strange trees, great ferns and plants which grew and died about 300 million years ago . Coal Is a valuable store of chemical energy which can be changed to give heat energy.

We need to get this fossil fuel so we can use its energy. This means cutting deep into the Earth which makes mining hard and dirty work. Miners face many dangers: polluted air, lung disease, fire, explosion, and roof collapse. There have to be safety precautions to protect miners.

Coal is formed from trees which grew millions of years ago. The trees died and fell into the swamp. Later the swamps disappeared and rocks formed over the top. The wood was squeezed by the weight and eventually turned into coal.

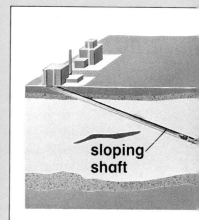

sloping
shaft

Miners now have machines to help them. The coal-cutting machines rip into the coal face freeing tonnes of coal as they move forward. The coal is piled on to conveyor belts which move it to the pit shaft, and then to the surface. Much of the coal goes straight to the power station. There it burns giving heat energy to make steam which drives dynamos to make electricity. The valuable chemicals in coal can be used to make plastics, nylon, fertilizers and paints.

Once miners had to use picks and shovels to dig coal. Nowadays huge machines cut into the coal face and deliver tonnes of coal on to conveyor belts.

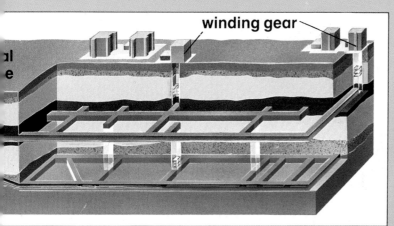

winding gear

This is a cross-section of a modern coal mine. The winding gear on the surface takes the miners down to the coal face. The coal leaves the mine by the sloping shaft.

15

Oil and gas

Oil is a very important energy source because it supplies such a lot of our energy. Oil is another fossil fuel which began to form hundreds of millions of years ago in swamps and shallow seas. Tiny animals and plants lived in these seas and died in the mud. They became buried under layers of rocks. As time passed, heat and pressure turned the animals into oil. Sometimes gas forms as well

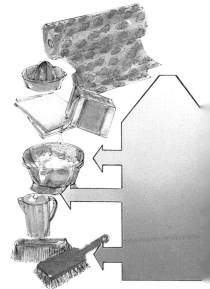

chemical factory

We obtain oil by drilling down through the rock layers, but first people must decide where to drill. Geologists are scientists who study rocks and they can suggest likely places to find oil. Some oil comes from the rocks under the sea bed. Drilling for oil is both expensive and dangerous.

Oil rigs for drilling at sea must be very strong. In bad weather waves batter the platform and could damage the rig.

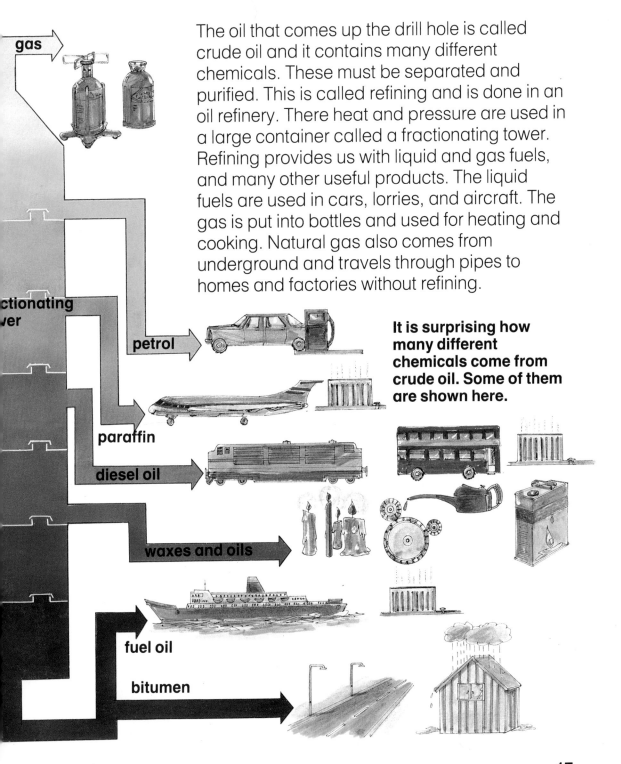

gas

The oil that comes up the drill hole is called crude oil and it contains many different chemicals. These must be separated and purified. This is called refining and is done in an oil refinery. There heat and pressure are used in a large container called a fractionating tower. Refining provides us with liquid and gas fuels, and many other useful products. The liquid fuels are used in cars, lorries, and aircraft. The gas is put into bottles and used for heating and cooking. Natural gas also comes from underground and travels through pipes to homes and factories without refining.

ctionating
ver

petrol

It is surprising how many different chemicals come from crude oil. Some of them are shown here.

paraffin

diesel oil

waxes and oils

fuel oil

bitumen

Nuclear fuel

In 1905 a very famous scientist called Albert Einstein amazed the world of science with a new idea. He said that enormous energy was locked inside the tiny pieces of matter called atoms. The centre of the atom is called the nucleus, and if the nucleus could be torn apart this energy would be set free.

After 50 years scientists had learnt how to control the energy from the nucleus. They had learnt how to release the energy more slowly. This slow release gives a steady supply of heat energy. In a nuclear power station the heat is used to make electricity.

Many people are concerned about the dangerous radiation which is released with the energy. They worry that a nuclear reactor might get out of control. The radiation might spread over a wide area, killing people or making them very ill.

Here is a simple picture of a uranium nucleus being split. This releases energy and is called a nuclear reaction.

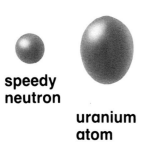

speedy neutron

uranium atom

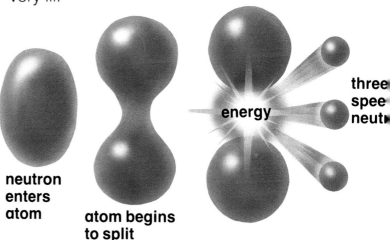

neutron enters atom

atom begins to split

energy

three spee neut

Another worry is how to get rid of the used fuel which still gives off dangerous radiation. Some is buried deep in the Earth and some under the sea in strong containers, but people wonder whether that is safe enough.

Nuclear scientists point out that nuclear power stations are very safe. Nobody has been killed at work in a nuclear power station. People are killed in coal mines and on oil rigs every year.

A nuclear power station is an enormous building made of concrete. Inside there is a container like a huge furnace where the nuclear reaction takes place. Water is pumped round pipes inside the furnace and turned into steam by the heat. The steam drives a dynamo to make electricity.

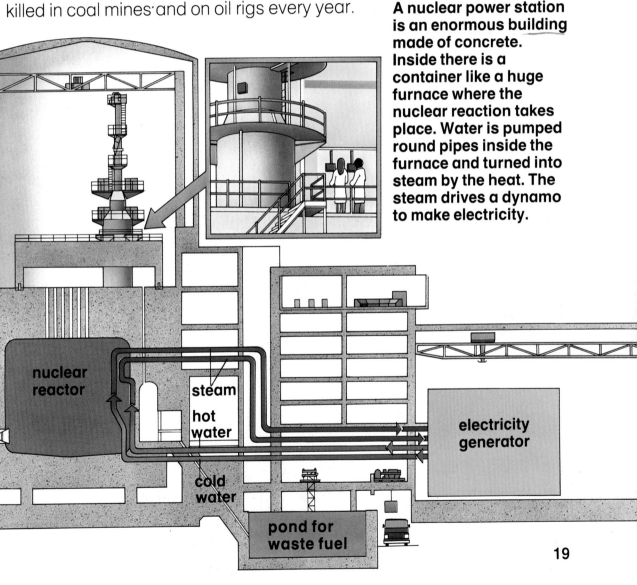

nuclear reactor

steam

hot water

cold water

electricity generator

pond for waste fuel

Running out

Oil, coal, gas, and nuclear fuels are running out. There is only a fixed amount of them in our planet Earth. We are using up these fuels very quickly. Experts try to predict how long they will last. It is possible that all the oil in our world could have gone by the time you are grown up. Coal will last longer (some say about 500 years). Nuclear fuels may last longer still.

How long fuels will really last depends on many things: how many people there will be in the world; how much energy they will use. More cities, more travel, and more machines mean more energy will be used. No energy means no electricity for light and heat, no fuel for cars, trains, aircraft, and other machines. Time is running out. What can we do?

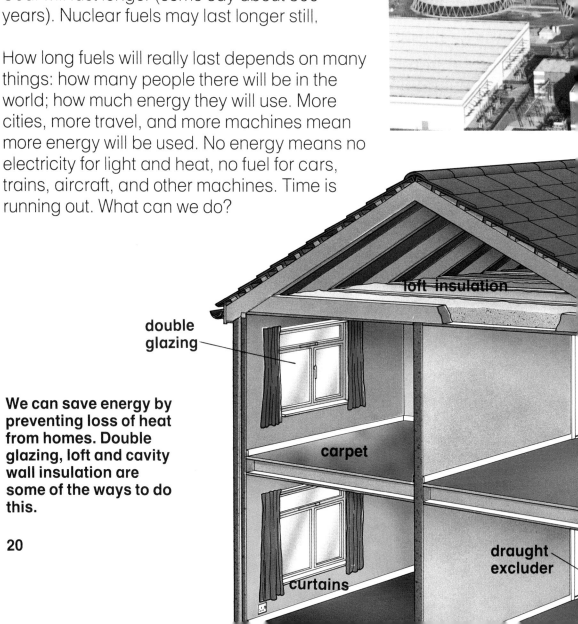

loft insulation

double glazing

carpet

We can save energy by preventing loss of heat from homes. Double glazing, loft and cavity wall insulation are some of the ways to do this.

draught excluder

curtains

20

Heat energy is wasted from cooling towers. It warms up the surrounding air and is lost. This energy could be used to warm homes. How else could we use it?

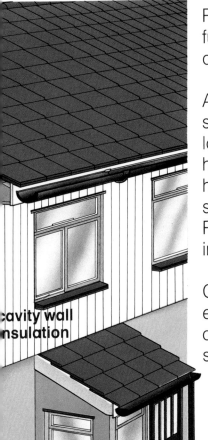

cavity wall insulation

Perhaps we can use less power and so make fuel stocks last longer. We can switch off lights and turn down heating. We can use less petrol.

A lot of heat energy is wasted from our homes, schools and workplaces. Cooling towers and large factories waste enormous amounts of heat energy which could be used to heat homes and greenhouses. Farmers burn stubble, and litter is dumped and buried. Perhaps we could turn these kinds of materials into fuel that we could use.

Our energy sources are running out fast, and even if we are very careful, the fossil fuels will one day be used up. We must look for new sources.

21

OTHER SOURCES

Sun and wind

Though our fossil fuels are running out, above us is the greatest energy source of all: the Sun! This energy will not be used up for thousands of millions of years. The energy from the Sun that reaches our Earth is 15,000 times more than all the energy we are using at the moment.

We can use the Sun's energy directly. The Sun's rays can be focused with a magnifying glass to make things very hot. The idea has been used in France where a solar furnace has been built. Large mirrors focus the Sun's rays on to the furnace. Another idea copies a greenhouse by fitting glass panels to the roofs of houses. Water in the panels gets hot and warms the house.

The Sun's energy heats the atmosphere, and makes the air rise. Cold air flows into the space underneath and causes a wind. Wind has been used for centuries to work machinery. We are now beginning to use wind machines again, but to make electricity. Using wind machines has drawbacks. The wind does not always blow: it can blow a gale or be a light breeze; and it changes direction. We need ways to store this unreliable energy. But wind energy is good because it is never used up and it is clean.

Windmills use the energy of moving air. These windmills make electricity for a ranch in California, USA. Thousands of windmills would be needed to make enough electricity for a city.

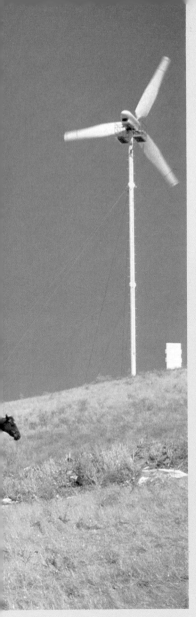

This solar furnace is 1600 metres up in the mountains in the south of France.

On the roof of this house in Switzerland solar panels store energy from the Sun. The energy is used to heat water for the house.

Water

The Sun's heat evaporates water from the sea and it later falls as rain on the hills inland. This rainwater has energy and it can do work when it flows in rivers down hill back to the sea. In the past water wheels used the moving water to drive machinery in mills and factories. The faster the water flows the more work it can do. In mountain areas many great dams have now been built to hold back millions of tonnes of water which can be used whenever it is needed. The water rushes through pipes and drives turbines which make electricity.

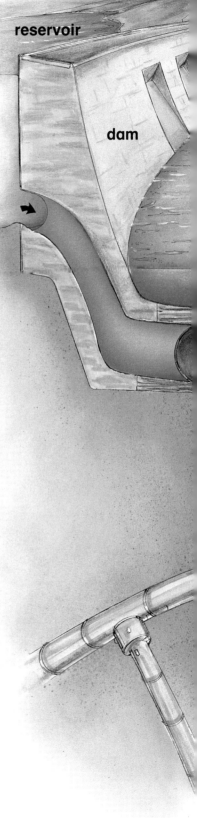

reservoir

dam

This power station on the River Rance in France uses the tide to make electricity.

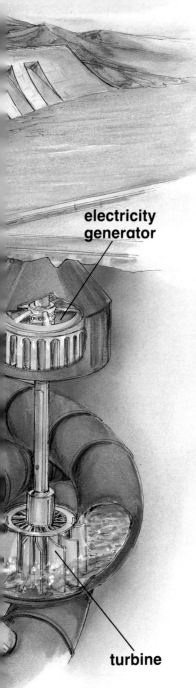

electricity generator

turbine

Swiftly moving water can turn a turbine and produce electricity.

This power station in Italy uses steam from the ground to make electricity.

Tides in the sea rise and fall each day. In some places there are very high tides. Near St Malo in France the tide rises by 10 metres and the tide water is trapped by a barrier built across the river mouth. The water is let in at high tide and let out at low tide when the flow drives turbines which make electricity. Could other river estuaries be used in this way?

Scientists are trying to obtain electrical energy from the moving waves of the sea, but there are problems. A power station which used the waves would need a structure several kilometres long. This would be difficult and expensive to build and could be a danger to shipping. There would be no pollution and the source could not be used up.

Food

The Sun is the source of all our energy (except nuclear energy). The Sun's energy is used by plants. They need it to grow. The green colouring, or chlorophyll, in the leaves uses the energy from the Sun to make food. It uses water from the roots, and carbon dioxide from the air, to make a sugar. This sugar is an energy store which plants use as food to make them grow. Animals eat plants to help them grow, and to provide the energy to move and keep warm.

There are thousands of leaves on a tree, and millions of plants in the world, all making food. That shows how important the Sun is.

The Sun's energy is needed to grow food for people and animals to eat. This food is their fuel.

You are full of energy. You walk, run, skip and jump, you keep warm. You are full of go. Where does all this go come from? You eat and drink food which gives you energy.

Here children are cycling. They enjoyed their breakfast of cereal, egg and orange juice. Energy in the food is stored in their muscles and then gives them the go to push the pedals. The stored energy in the food fuel is changed to energy of movement.

Foods that contain sugar and starch are a big source of energy. They include sweets, bread, potatoes, pasta, and rice. Some of us eat more of these kinds of food than we need. Our bodies change them into fat and store them.

These children use their energy to keep alive, to keep warm and to pedal their bicycles. They get their energy from their food. The energy to grow the food comes from the Sun.

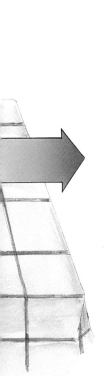

In the future

Because our fossil fuels are running out fast we need to search for new energy sources. Wind, water, and plants are some possible sources but there are others, too.

Deep inside the Earth the rocks are very very hot. People are trying to find ways of using this heat. Engineers are drilling down 5 kilometres into the Earth at Penryn in Cornwall. They hope to pump down water and pump up steam. The steam could be used for heating, or to make electricity.

Water is pumped down into the Earth. The hot rocks heat the water which then rises to the surface and is used to make electricity. Or, it can be used directly to heat homes or hospitals.

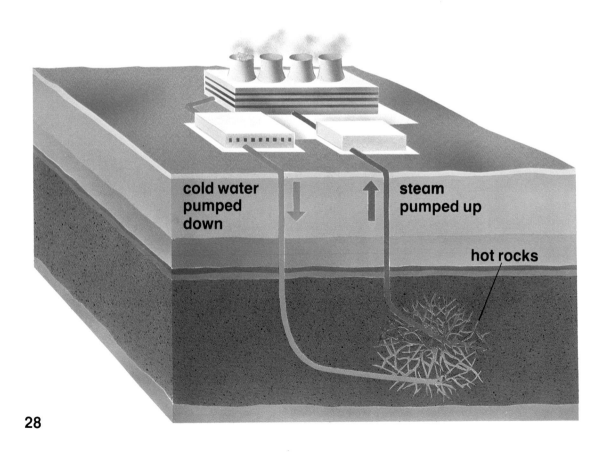

cold water pumped down

steam pumped up

hot rocks

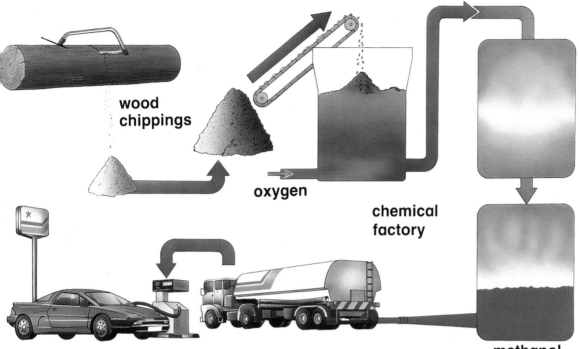

wood chippings

oxygen

chemical factory

methanol

Plants and trees are great collectors of energy. Plants that grew millions of years ago have now turned into coal, but a million years seems a long time to wait. Perhaps we can use the plants' energy sooner.

In some parts of the world energy crops are grown. Energy crops are quick growing trees, or plants that can be made into fuel. Waste paper and sawdust can also be made into fuel bricks. Some farmers use animal and plant waste to produce electricity for their farms.

Perhaps one day people will use the Sun's energy directly, to produce electricity on a large scale. Do you have any ideas for new sources of energy?

Waste wood chippings can be used to make fuel. The wood chips are changed in a chemical factory. They are changed to methanol. This can be used instead of petrol in motor cars.

GLOSSARY, BOOKS TO READ

A glossary is a word list. This one explains unusual words that are used in this book.

Atom The smallest bit of something. If you divide an atom you no longer have the same material.

Atmosphere The envelope of air around the Earth. It contains a mixture of gases but mainly carbon dioxide, oxygen, and nitrogen.

Carbon dioxide A gas found in the air which has no colour and no smell. It is given out when living things breathe, and often forms when things burn.

Cavity wall Walls of brick houses are often built with a space in the middle to make the houses warmer and drier.

Chlorophyll The green colouring matter in plants.

Conveyor belt A machine with a long moving belt which can carry material from one place to another.

Double glazing A way of lessening the loss of heat through windows. Two layers of glass replace the usual one layer.

Dynamo A machine that changes mechanical or moving energy into electrical energy.

Estuary The wide part of a river where it meets the sea. As the tide in the sea rises and falls water flows in and out of the estuary.

Generator A machine which turns mechanical energy into electrical energy.

Fractionating tower A tall vertical container in which a mixture of liquids is separated.

Fossil fuel An energy source made from plants or animals which died long ago.

Insulation A means of lessening the passage of heat.

Methanol A liquid like alcohol which is poisonous but which could replace petrol as fuel in cars.

Nucleus The central part of an atom which contains most of the mass. If the nucleus of a uranium atom is split a lot of heat energy and radiation are given out.

Pollution Spoiling or poisoning of land, water, or air with rubbish or waste.

Radiation Rays or particles which are given out when the nucleus of an atom is split. It can be very harmful and can take many years to die away.

Solar panel A glass panel which is fixed to the roof of a house to capture energy from the Sun.

Turbine A motor which turns when water or gas push against blades on a wheel.

BOOKS TO READ
You can find out more about fuels and energy by reading some of these books. Most of them are harder than this one, but they all have good pictures.

Energy, Desmond Boyle, Macdonald, 1980.
Mines and mining, New Reference Library, Macdonald, 1979.
Nuclear Energy, Nigel Hawkes, Franklin Watts, 1981.
Oil, New Reference Library, Macdonald, 1979.